ROAD TRAVEL

Angela Royston

Macdonald Educational

How to use this book

First, look at the contents page opposite. Read the chapter list to see if it includes the subject you want. The list tells you what each page is about. You can then find the page with the information you need.

If you want to know about one particular thing, look it up in the index on page 31. For example, if you want to know about taxis, the index tells you that there is something about them on page 12. The index also lists the pictures in the book.

When you read this book, you will find some unusual words. The glossary on page 30 explains what they mean.

Series Editor
Margaret Conroy

Book Editor
John Morton

Production
Marguerite Fenn

Factual Adviser
John Stevenson

Reading Consultant
Amy Gibbs

Series Design
Robert Mathias/Anne Isseyegh

Book Design
Julia Osorno

Teacher Panel
Ieuan Bishop, Catherine Daniel, Bernadette Hill

Illustrations
Graham Thompson

Photographs
City Mobile Ltd.: 29
Robert Harding Picture Library: 16, 23
Hutchison Library: 15, 17
Macdonald Library: 11L/Ford Motor Co.: 26
Morgan Motor Co. Ltd./COI: 26–27
Rex Features/Sipa: 19, 21B
Scania (GB) Limited (Scania P112H 6×2): 21T
Spectrum Colour Library: cover
Toyota: 27
ZEFA: 7, 11R, 12L & R, 25

CONTENTS

ROADS

From dirt track to motorway

This book is about roads and the many vehicles which use them. Cars, trucks, buses and bikes make travelling quicker and easier, but they all need roads to drive along. We use roads to go to school, to visit friends, or to move huge loads to faraway cities.

The pictures show many roads of different sizes. Farmers use narrow, winding country lanes to move animals, hay or vegetables. Long ago, most roads were bumpy lanes which turned to mud when it rained. Nowadays bigger, straighter roads link towns and cities.

The village below is jammed with noisy traffic. Most of the traffic is trying to get to a city. The other picture shows the same village after a motorway was built past it. Do you think the motorway makes the village a better place to live in?

A street in Afghanistan. Most roads in the world are dirt tracks, and are used by people walking or riding animals. Strong animals like oxen can also pull heavy carts. Animals cost less to buy than trucks or cars, and can also do farmwork for their owners.

The biggest roads of all are the motorways which bypass towns and sweep across the countryside. Motorways carry huge amounts of traffic, but they are very expensive to build. Cuttings have to be blasted through hills, and forests cut down to make way for them. They are also expensive to keep in repair. In some countries drivers pay a toll or tax to use motorways, and this helps to pay for the cost.

Building roads

Enormous trucks and streams of cars roar along our busiest roads day and night. After a while the road surface breaks up and has to be repaired. In cold countries many roads also have to be repaired after winter because snow and ice have cracked them, and this may mean they have to be closed for a time.

Not all roadworks are for repairs. Straighter, wider roads speed our journeys and prevent traffic jams at the busiest times. Dirt roads may take a lot of traffic but finally have to be tarred over to take even more traffic. Corners on roads may be straightened, narrow roads widened to take extra lanes of traffic, and sometimes a flyover is built to take one road high over another busy road.

Roads cost a lot of money to build because so many people and machines are needed to build them. Many layers make the road strong enough to carry heavy traffic.

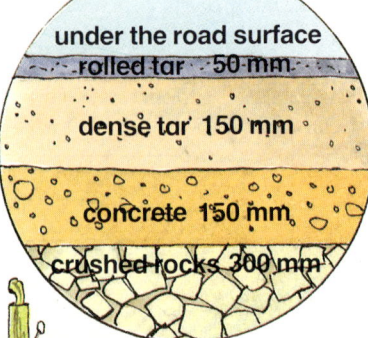

under the road surface
rolled tar   50 mm
dense tar 150 mm
concrete 150 mm
crushed rocks 300 mm

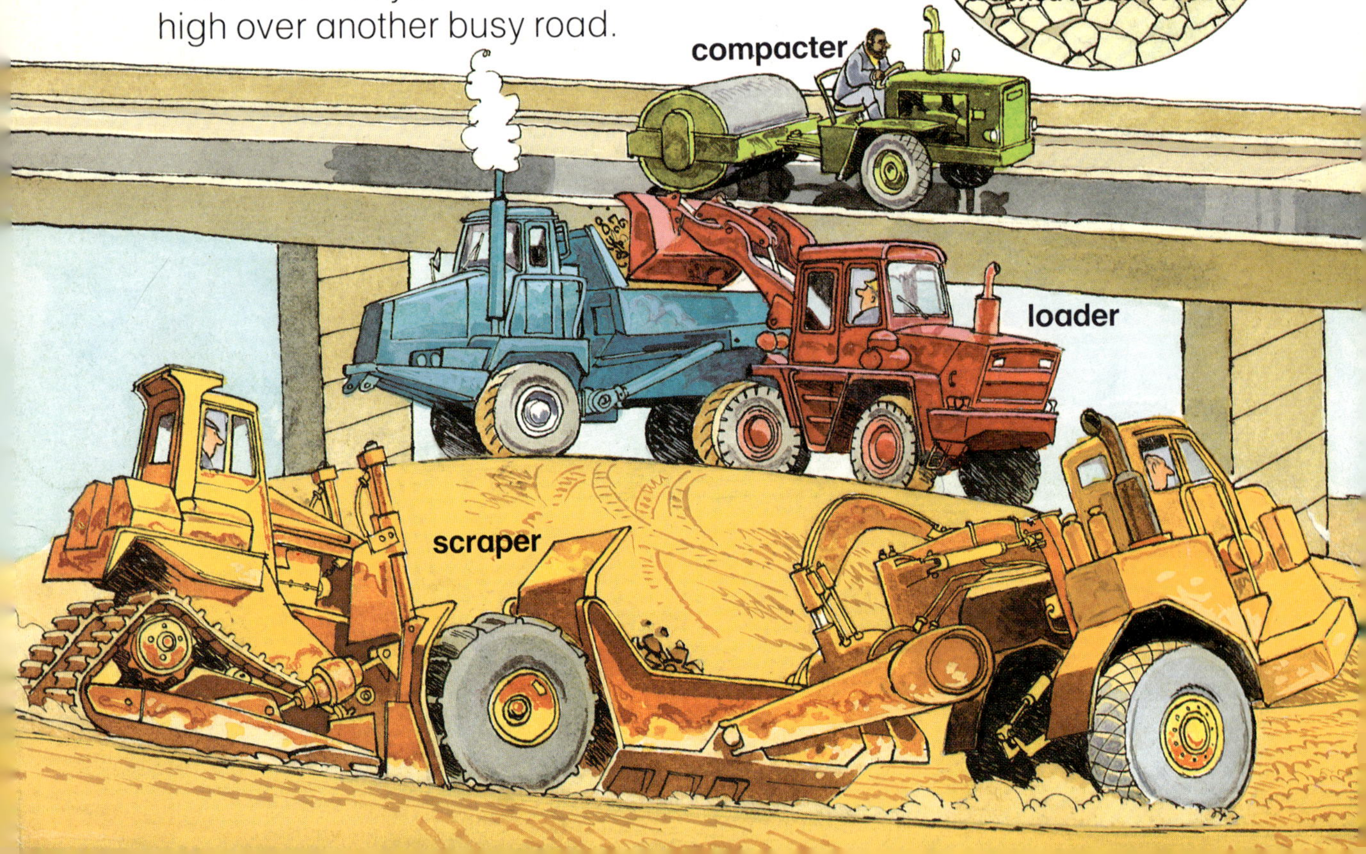

compacter

loader

scraper

The shortest routes between major cities are motorways. They have many lanes, but few traffic lights or other hold-ups, so they are quicker and easier to drive on than ordinary roads. As more and more cars and trucks use the roads, more and more motorways are built, but fast new motorways encourage even more people to make long car journeys.

Some people think that we have too many roads and vehicles. Do you think that it would be better if more people and goods went by train, which is a faster, safer, and often cheaper way to travel? The problem is that while roads go all over the country and can reach almost every house, shop or office, trains only run along a few well-used lines. Railways are best for moving heavy loads such as coal, which can be moved straight from the mines to the power stations. Underground trains help keep cars off busy city roads.

Bridges are even more expensive to build than roads. There are several different types of bridge. The one over the river is a suspension bridge and the other one is a beam bridge.

paver

dump truck

bulldozer

Controlling the traffic

What would happen if there were no signs or laws to control traffic? People would be able to drive as fast as they liked, park where they liked, and there would be many traffic jams and accidents. Strict traffic laws make driving quicker, easier, and safer. Even so, over 200,000 people are killed in road accidents each year. This means that someone dies somewhere in the world every 2½ minutes.

Driving tests help to make the roads safer. People are not allowed to drive cars or ride motorbikes without passing a driving test to make sure they can drive well and can understand the traffic rules and road signs. Then they get a driving licence. Bus and truck drivers have to pass special tests which are more difficult.

Road signs help you find your way. They tell you how fast you can drive and where you may park or may not park. At zebra crossings, drivers must stop and let people cross. Roundabouts and traffic lights control the flow of traffic where several roads meet.

Many road signs are the same all over the world. Signs in a red triangle warn of dangers. Those in circles give orders. What do you think each of these signs means?

Sometimes a broken down truck or an accident causes a traffic jam. Some cities have cameras to watch out for jams, with traffic controllers in special centres watching television sets to see where there is trouble. Traffic police are sent to get the traffic moving again, and may tell vehicles to take another route. Many cities, particularly in North America, have been specially planned to avoid traffic jams by having huge highways criss-crossing the cities. Do you think that's a good idea, or do they make the cities noisy and ugly?

Drivers in Tokyo use this flyover to avoid narrow streets and traffic jams. But people who live near roads like this have to put up with a lot of noise and dirt.

In some places, like this old English street, cars are not allowed so that shoppers can walk in safety. Can you think of another reason for not allowing cars and heavy trucks in this street?

CARRYING PEOPLE

Cars

How many of your friends go to school by car? If we go somewhere by car, we make up our own minds when to leave, and if it rains, we'll stay warm and dry in our car. We can park near where we want to go so we won't have a long wet walk from a bus stop or railway station.

This makes cars seem the best way to travel. But suppose you get stuck in a traffic jam, or can't find a parking place? Car travel can take longer than going by bus or train. It can also be less safe and more tiring, especially on long journeys or in bad weather.

People without a car can hire a taxi to take them wherever they want to go. These German taxis are white so they are easy to see. In some countries taxis are pulled by horses, or someone on a bike. The photo on the left shows Delhi, in India. How many ways of carrying people can you see in it?

Cars are expensive to buy and run. The people who build cars try to make them reliable, but all cars need repairs. Petrol is expensive. This is partly because the world's suppy of oil, which is used to make petrol, is running low. Modern cars are designed to use less petrol.

Small amounts of lead in petrol make engines run better. But lead is poisonous, and breathing the exhaust fumes can be unhealthy. Many countries ban the use of lead in petrol.

Cars have changed the way people live. Most people in North America have cars. People go to shopping centres where they can buy all they need for a week or more. People without cars could not carry this amount of shopping so they must live nearer the shops and shop more often. When people have cars they can drive further to work, so offices or factories can be built outside the towns where their workers live.

Put an egg in a wooden box. Hit the box so it shoots forward. The egg rolls and smashes on the box end. Now tape down the egg in a wooden box glued into a cardboard box. If you hit the box, it crumples, leaving the egg safe and sound.

The same idea is used in cars. The car body around the passengers is extra strong, but the front and back are less strong. Passengers are strapped in with safety belts. If the car is hit, its front or back crumples, protecting the passengers.

Bikes and motorbikes

Riding a bicycle is good exercise and is cheap. It is often quicker, too, as cars can get stuck in traffic jams, but people on bikes can cut through the lines of slow-moving cars or buses.

Motorbikes can be exciting to ride. But they are very dangerous, and you must wear proper clothing to protect you. Bright markings and lights help other drivers see you.

Riding a bike in bad weather isn't always easy, comfortable, or safe. In rain you may get soaked. You cannot see clearly and the roads are slippery. Motorcyclists must wear heavy, waterproof clothes to keep them warm and dry in bad weather.

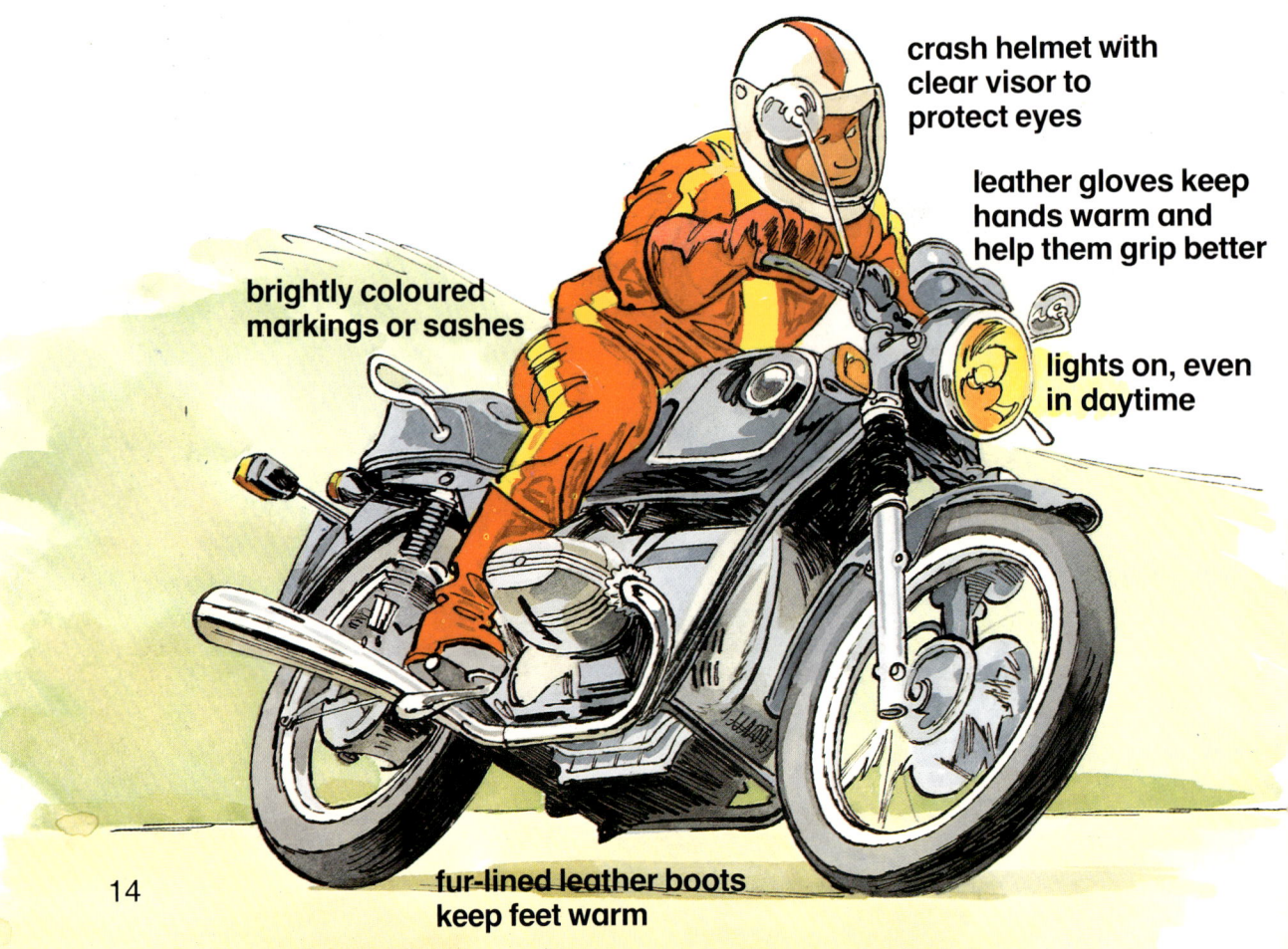

crash helmet with clear visor to protect eyes

leather gloves keep hands warm and help them grip better

brightly coloured markings or sashes

lights on, even in daytime

fur-lined leather boots keep feet warm

Riding a bike or motorbike can be dangerous. Bikes are much narrower than cars so car or truck drivers often do not notice them. Some cities have special cycle lanes where only cyclists can ride. This makes cycling much safer, but most roads are not wide enough for bike lanes. Many countries have laws to make motorcyclists wear crash helmets, which protect their heads in accidents.

Bikes only have small storage boxes or baskets. But in many cities motorbike riders carry urgent letters or parcels from one office to another. This is far quicker than sending parcels by car or van.

Motorbikes can carry no more than two people unless they have a sidecar, but they are much cheaper to buy and run than cars. A 350 cc motorbike can go more than 20 kilometres on one litre of petrol. Most cars can only go about ten kilometres on one litre of fuel.

Rush-hour in Beijing, China. Most people in Chinese cities use bicycles to get to work. Do you think this is a good idea?

Buses and trams

In Asia and Africa buses are usually crammed with people and luggage. The bus is shared by many people and so it is cheap. In Europe and North America many people prefer to go by car, but most cars have only one or two people in them. Too many cars on the roads cause traffic jams. How would you persuade people to leave their cars at home and travel by bus?

A village bus in Pakistan. In many parts of the world buses are the most popular way to travel, particularly where few people can afford a car and there isn't a good railway service.

A good, fast service may encourage people to go by bus instead of by car. In some countries the government pays part of the cost of running the buses to keep fares low. Some cities have special bus lanes to allow buses to speed along busy roads, avoiding the other traffic.

In the country there are less people than in the cities. Children often have to go a long way to get to school or the shops. In some parts there are not enough people to pay the cost of running a bus. Do you think the government should help pay to run these buses? Some countries use post-buses which carry passengers and also deliver letters.

Electric trams are cheaper to run than buses. Trams get electricity from overhead wires and travel on smooth rails like railway lines, so they use less power than buses. But trams can only go where the rails go, and the rails take up a lot of road space and may cause jams.

Dutch trams in Amsterdam run through the city centre alongside other traffic. Many European cities have regular tram services with cheap fares.

If each car below carries just two people, all those people could be seated in the two buses. How often do you see a car with just *one* person in it?

double-decker bus

articulated bus

CARRYING GOODS

Trucks and vans

Nearly everything in your home was brought by truck or van. Even the bricks, plaster, tiles and wood came by truck. The cooker was taken from the factory to a shop in a big truck. The television was probably delivered by van.

A truck's weight is carried on its axles and wheels. Many axles have two wheels at each end. Some trucks have 16 or more wheels in all. The more wheels a truck has, the less weight each wheel must carry. Heavy trucks with only a few wheels will damage roads.

Vans and lorries are called commercial vehicles because they are mostly owned by companies and businesses. Look at the names of the companies and goods advertised on the sides of trucks. Companies choose the size and type of van or truck to suit their load. Small vans are often used by shopkeepers for delivering to local houses and offices. They are also used by plumbers, electricians and other tradespeople.

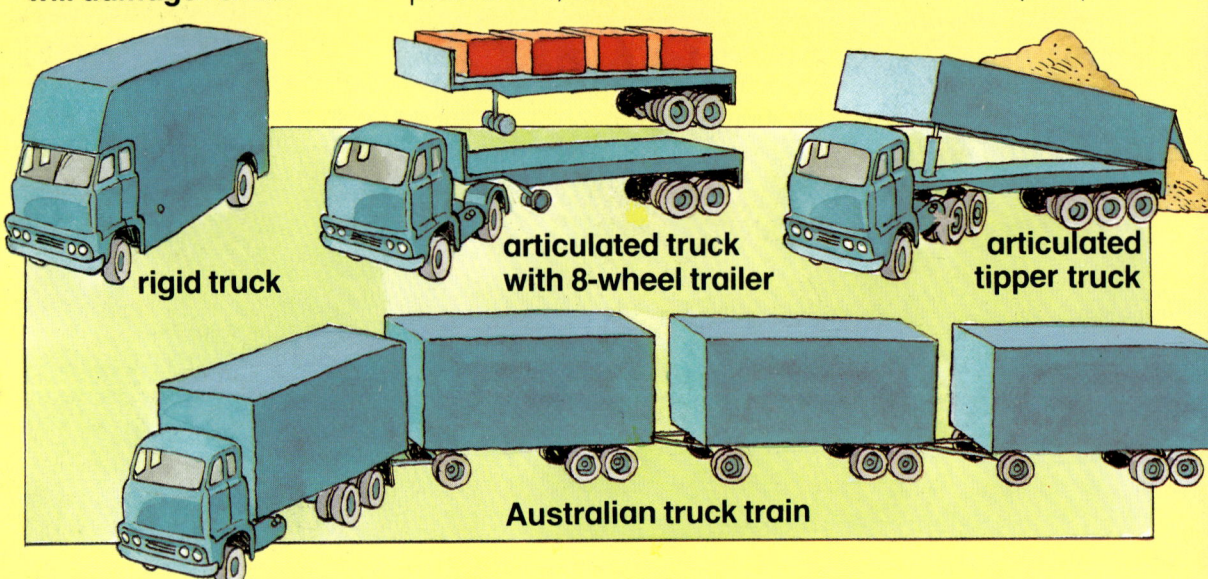

rigid truck

articulated truck
with 8-wheel trailer

articulated
tipper truck

Australian truck train

Trucks crossing the Sahara Desert. Trucks can go almost anywhere, not only across deserts and over mountain passes, but to almost every city back street.

There are two main types of lorry – rigid and articulated. Rigid trucks have a frame in one piece. But if rigid trucks are too long they are difficult to steer round tight corners. Articulated trucks have two parts – the cab and trailer are separate. In Britain articulated trucks can be as long as 15 metres, and even longer in other countries. The longer the truck and the heavier the load, the more wheels are needed to carry the load.

In Australia several trailers are sometimes joined together. These truck trains run on special roads to take goods across this vast country. Australia has few railways, and truck trains carry bulky goods usually taken by trains in other countries.

Many people think trucks are often too big and noisy for the old narrow streets of towns and villages. But trucks are the easiest way to carry most things. Before trucks were used, many goods went by railway or canal. Although Britain still has many canals and railway lines, nearly all goods are now taken by road.

Driving a truck

A tachograph records on a disk card how far a truck travels, for how long, and at what speeds. Many countries have laws to stop people driving trucks for too long without a break. This makes sure that drivers do not get too tired to drive safely.

Driving a truck used to be hard, noisy work. Modern trucks are easier to drive because they have power-assisted steering and brakes, and cabs specially made to keep out engine noise. Trucks have many more gears than cars. They help the engine to haul huge loads up hills and reach speeds of 100 kilometres an hour.

There is more to being a truck driver than just driving a truck. A driver cleans the trailer and connects it to the cab before starting off. Then the driver joins up the electric cables that power the lights and brakes. The driver also tops up the oil and water and fills the 400-litre diesel fuel tank. Finally, the driver checks the documents for the journey. Some trucks travel through many countries, so drivers need passports, road maps, different money for each country, and other special documents.

A driver plans when to stop to eat or sleep. Some cabs' insides are almost like small caravans, and may have a sink, fridge, and stove for drivers to cook their own meals. But long distance truck-driving is lonely work. Drivers often eat in transport cafes where they can swap information on traffic hold-ups or weather conditions with other drivers. More and more drivers use CB radio to talk to each other as they drive along. At night the driver can sleep in a bunk at the back of the cab.

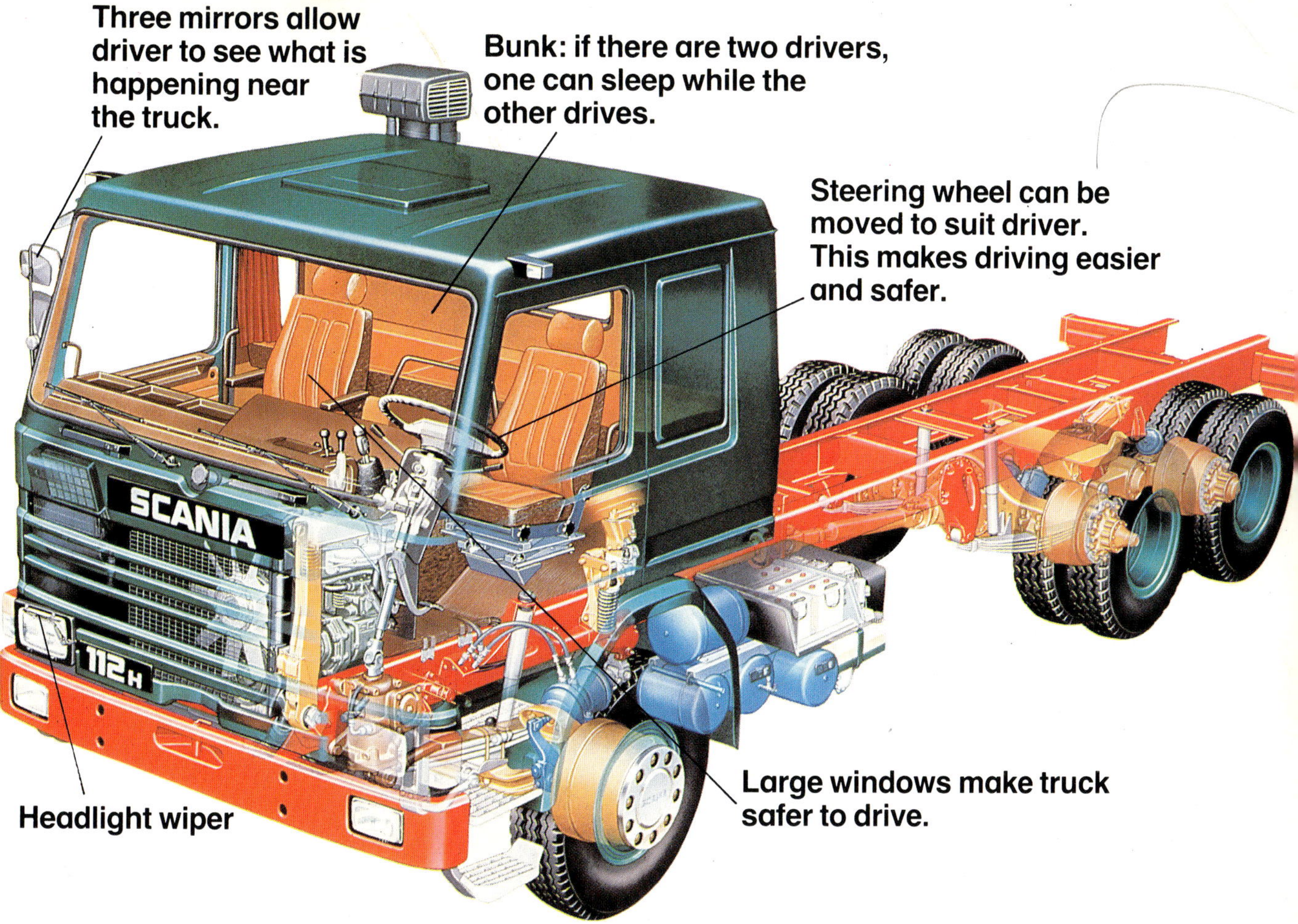

Three mirrors allow driver to see what is happening near the truck.

Bunk: if there are two drivers, one can sleep while the other drives.

Steering wheel can be moved to suit driver. This makes driving easier and safer.

SCANIA

112 H

Headlight wiper

Large windows make truck safer to drive.

Some things that make truck-driving safer and more comfortable. The powerful engine is under the cab, which tilts forward to make the engine easy to reach.

This truck driver comes from Pakistan. Many drivers decorate their cabs with religious pictures, family photos or special mascots. Why do you think they do this?

Special trucks and vans

Trucks can be built to do many things. Snow ploughs, for example, push snow off the road, and special trucks spread sand on icy roads. Fire engines and ambulances are always ready to deal with emergencies, and can quickly get to the scene of any accident. Trucks can carry all kinds of loads – cars, cranes or animals. Huge pieces of machinery can be taken to pieces and carried bit by bit.

These trucks all have a special use.

A fire engine's hose and ladder are powered by the engine.

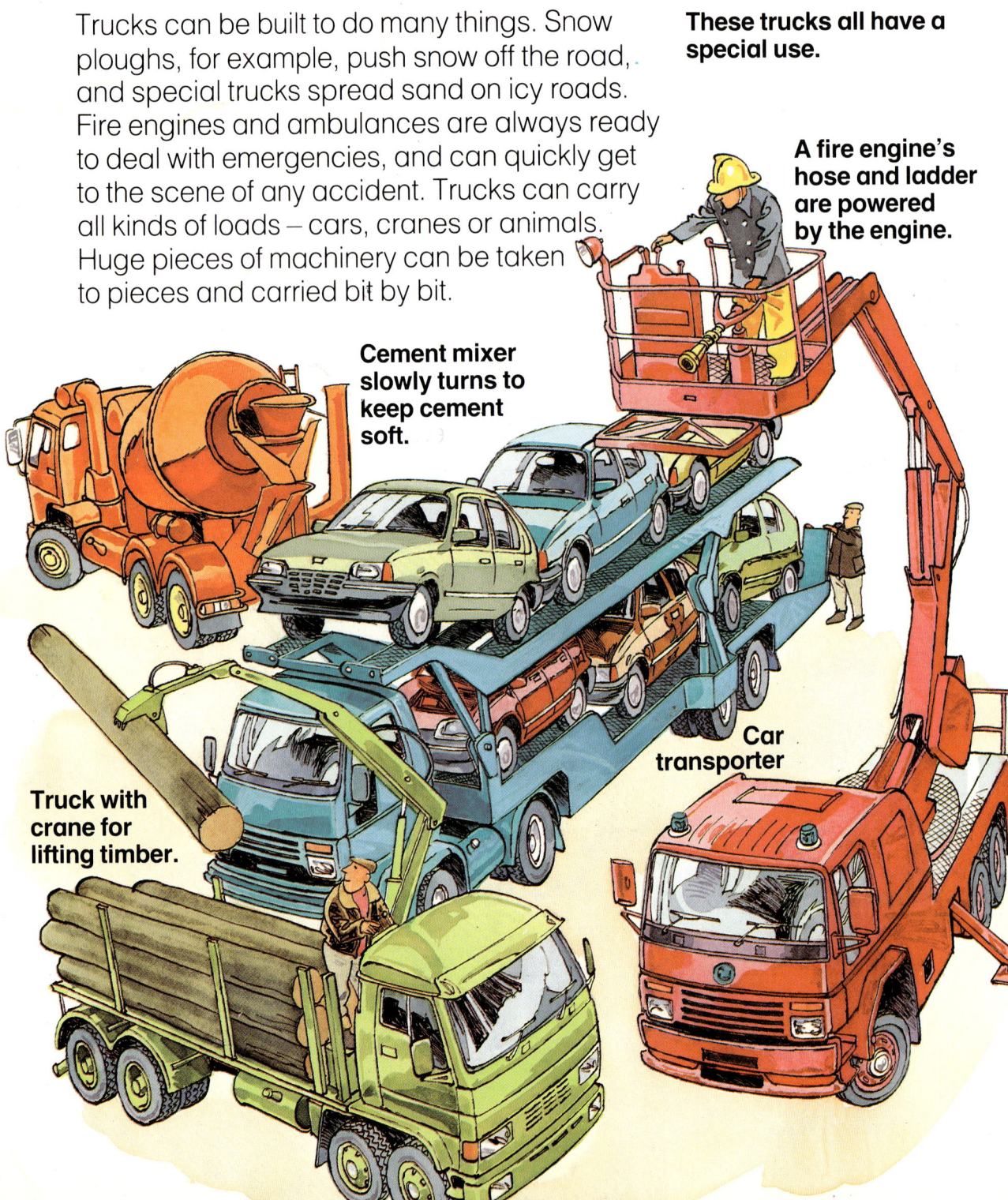

Cement mixer slowly turns to keep cement soft.

Truck with crane for lifting timber.

Car transporter

Trucks can move liquids, like milk or petrol, in bottles or barrels. But a tanker is the best way to move liquids as no space is wasted between the bottles or barrels, and the liquid can be easily unloaded with a hose pipe into a filling station or bottling factory. Tankers are divided into compartments which stop the huge weight of liquid splashing backwards or forwards when the truck stops. Tankers also carry dry things like sugar or cement powder.

Meat, butter and cheese last longer in a fridge, so some trucks are like huge fridges on wheels, keeping food chilled as they travel. Frozen foods like ice cream are kept even colder.

Coal, sand, and other loose loads are moved in tippers or dumpers. To empty them, a rod pushes up and tilts the part that stores the load. Dumping in places like building sites is a lot easier and quicker than unloading with shovels.

Some loads are too big to travel by rail. Trucks can carry almost anything – even a house! Truck drivers with loads as big as this need the help of the police, who decide which route the truck should take, and often drive in front of and behind the truck to warn other traffic.

23

Under the bonnet

A little more than a hundred years ago there were no cars. The first petrol-driven car was built in 1886 by Karl Benz, a German inventor. A modern car has the same type of engine but it works much better. Car makers are always trying to build engines that last longer and make more power from less fuel.

Karl Benz's engine was driven by internal combustion, which means 'burning inside'. These engines make power from tiny explosions in the cylinders. In.petrol engines sparkplugs light the fuel. In diesel engines fuel is squirted straight into the cylinders. The air in the cylinders is squeezed, becomes hot, and lights the fuel. Diesel engines make more power from less fuel and are cheaper to run. They are used in some cars and most trucks and buses.

Petrol and diesel are made from oil, which is expensive. Scientists are trying to design battery-powered cars and trucks because electric engines are cheap, quiet, and clean. But they are not powerful and can not travel at high speeds. They do not run for long before their batteries run down and have to be recharged with electricity. Batteries are also very heavy and take up a lot of space.

What is this battery-powered van being used for? Do you think a diesel engine would be as good for this job?

The main parts of a car

The carburettor mixes the right amount of air and petrol to enter each cylinder.

The spark plugs set alight the petrol and air in the cylinders.

Burning fuel forces the pistons down in the cylinders, which turn the crankshaft.

The crankshaft turns the propeller shaft.

The clutch allows the driver to change from one gear to another.

The gears match the engine's speed to the wheels' speed.

electric
engine

batteries

Los Angeles, USA, often lies under a poisonous layer of smog. Smog is a mixture of fog and smoke, or exhaust fumes. The fumes are gases left over when petrol or diesel burns in an engine.

The battery provides electricity to start the engine and work things like lights.

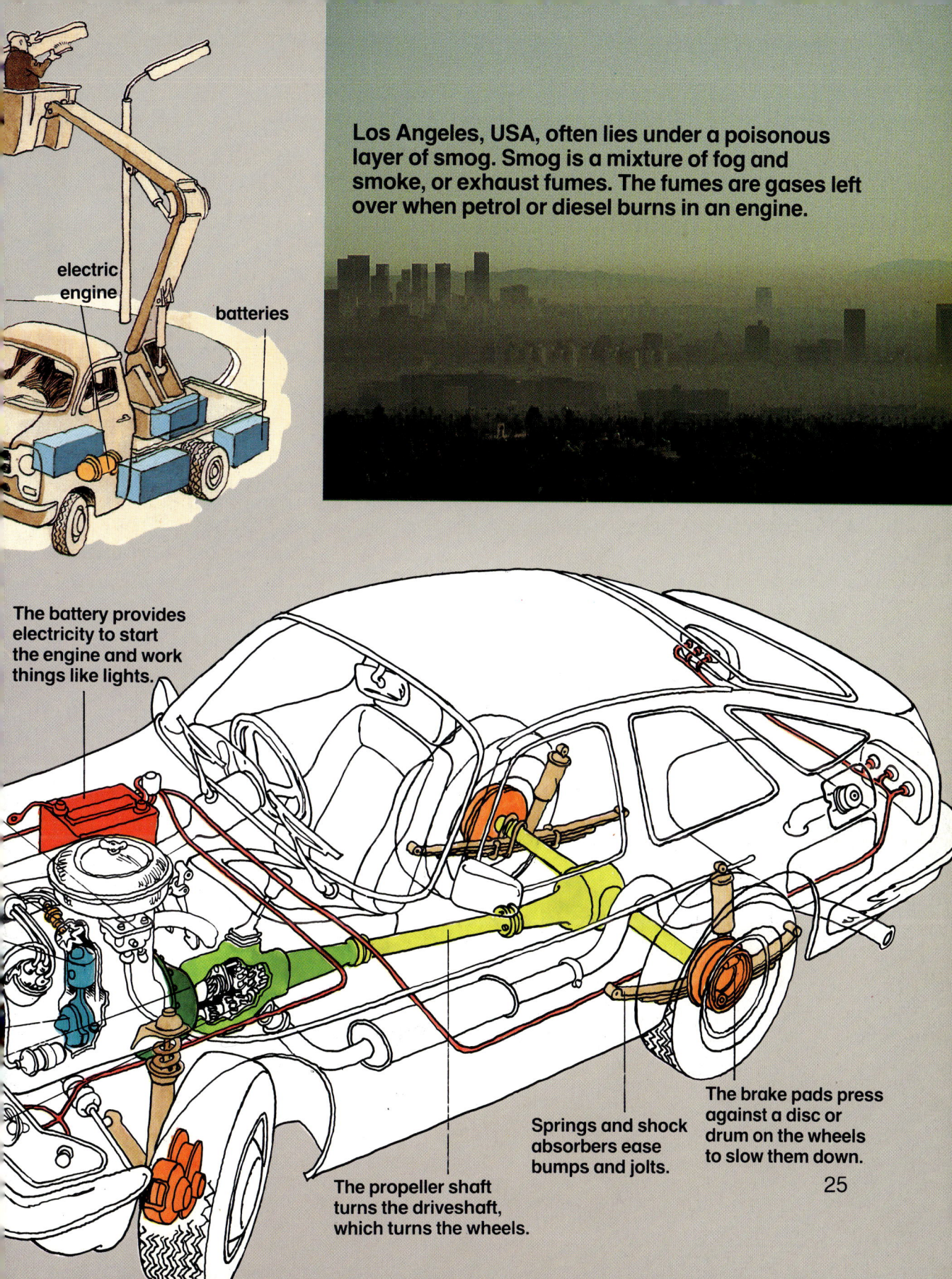

The brake pads press against a disc or drum on the wheels to slow them down.

Springs and shock absorbers ease bumps and jolts.

The propeller shaft turns the driveshaft, which turns the wheels.

25

How a car is made

For many years only rich people could afford cars. They were expensive because they were built by hand, one by one. Rolls-Royces and some other luxury cars are still made this way. An American called Henry Ford was the first person to mass-produce cheap cars, by using an assembly line. Thousands of parts all exactly the same are brought to the factory. A moving belt carries the car frames and pieces are added as the frames go by. Bit by bit, thousands of identical cars are assembled.

Today many makes of car are assembled by robots rather than by people. Although robots are expensive to buy, they cut costs as fewer people have to be paid wages. Thousands of people still work for companies that make parts, such as tyres or light bulbs, which are used on car assembly lines.

Expensive sports cars in this English factory are still made by hand, just as the very first cars were. Each car takes about 11 weeks to make.

A Ford car factory in 1928. Each worker has a special job to do to the cars as they go by on the assembly line. Each worker does the same job day in and day out. Henry Ford made the first cars that were cheap enough for ordinary people to buy.

It costs a lot of money to build an assembly line for a new design of car, and only the richest companies can afford to do it. A few very big companies build nearly all the cars in the world. Some cars use parts made in one country, such as Spain or Japan, which are assembled in another, such as Britain or Germany.

A Japanese robot assembly line in 1986. Robots make fewer mistakes than people, but they take away jobs from car-workers. A robot assembly line can make a car in as little as 11 hours.

Recent improvements

New cars made by different companies often look rather similar. This is because the people who design cars want to improve the old designs in the same ways. They want cars to be safer and more comfortable, and they want them to run better and more cheaply. Designers try to make their cars better and more reliable because they hope more people will buy them.

Building a new car costs a lot of money. Car designers use wind tunnels to make sure that the air will flow smoothly around a car and not slow it down too much. Computers help designers try experiments with new ideas and shapes.

Petrol in America is cheaper than in Europe. Because of this, most American cars are much bigger. Even so, American car makers are building smaller cars that use less petrol because the price of petrol has gone up so much in the last ten years or so. This is a 1954 Cadillac. People often call these large cars 'gas-guzzlers' – gas is the American word for petrol.

Computers are also being used inside cars. Some warn you if your car is too close to the car in front, and may even automatically apply the brakes to slow your car down. Other computers can tell you which route to take. Computers can also make sure that exactly the correct amount of fuel reaches the engine, wasting none of the expensive petrol or diesel.

One improvement for cars is turbocharged engines. These use the exhaust gases to drive a turbine. This works like a tiny windmill, with hundreds of blades which are spun round by the gases. A turbine helps the engine make more power from less fuel.

You might see many more cars as small as this British two-person car in the future. As petrol becomes more expensive, people will want cars that are cheap to run and waste no space. This car travels as far on a litre of petrol as many motorbikes, but is much safer than a motorbike. It has three wheels and an automatic tilting system to help it turn corners.

GLOSSARY, BOOKS TO READ

A glossary is a word list. This one explains unusual words that are used in this book.

Articulated An articulated bus or truck has two or more parts to its body. The parts are joined together but are free to move in different directions.

Assembly line A moving line of cars being built. Each worker has a special job to do on the line, to help build the cars as they go past.

Carburettor A carburettor mixes air with petrol and sprays it in a very fine mist into the cylinders, where the mixture burns. There must be exactly the right amount of air and petrol, or the engine will not work well.

CB radio Citizen's Band radio allows drivers to talk to each other on small radio transmitters and receivers that only work on special radio frequencies.

Crankshaft A rod that is bent, or cranked, so that it can be connected to all the pistons. The crankshaft turns the up and down movement of the pistons into a movement that goes round and round, and can turn the wheels.

Diesel A fuel that is cheaper and safer to use than petrol. But diesel engines are heavier than petrol engines, and this is one reason why most cars have petrol engines. Diesel engines also make dirtier exhaust fumes.

Mass-production Making thousands of cars as cheaply as possible. Each person who works in a factory which uses mass-production has one special job to do. One job, for example, might be fixing seats to the car. Workers do nothing but their own special jobs so that they learn to do them very quickly. Special machines are also used to help make cars. The same idea is used to make all sorts of different things, such as cameras, radios, or cakes.

Smog Smog is found in many parts of the world where there are lots of vehicles and smoky factories. Smog is sometimes trapped over a city and is very unpleasant and dangerous.

Tachograph A tachograph records on a circular piece of card the time of day, the truck's speed, and for how long the driver stops. Many countries have laws to make truck or long-distance bus drivers use this instrument. Some people call the tachograph a 'spy in the cab'.

Vehicle Anything with wheels that runs on roads and carries something.

BOOKS TO READ

You can find out more about road travel in these books.

Getting About in Towns by Paul White, Adam and Charles Black, 1984

Transport and Travel by Frances Wilkins, Batsford, 1985

Cars and Trucks by John Fletcher, Kingfisher, 1982

Looking at Cars, **Looking at Buses**, **Looking at Trucks**, and **Looking at Motorbikes**, all by Cliff Lines, Wayland, 1984

How it Works, **The Motor Car** by David Carey, Ladybird, 1965